Spying

Henry Brook

Illustrated by Staz Johnson and Adrian Roots
Designed by Helen Edmonds, Anna Gould and Will Dawes

Edited by Alex Frith

Spying expert: Terry Charman, senior historian, Imperial War Museum

Contents

4   Tell me a secret...

6   Going underground

12   Over the hill

16   Secret messages

18   Letters in disguise

22   Spies of the ancient world

24   Lord of the spies

26   Spy detectives

28   Intelligence on tap

30   Spies at war

36   Global espionage

38   The Second World War

42   Secret languages

46   Mind games

48   Old friends, new enemies

52   Circles of deceit

54   CIA around the world

58   Captured!

62   Robot spies

66   Behind enemy lines

68   Countering terrorism

70   Risky business

74   Truth and fiction

76   Glossary

78   Index and Acknowledgements

Cover photo: A US soldier with night vision enhancer goggles ready for a reconnaissance mission in the desert

A surveillance officer tails a suspect through a hole in his newspaper.

Tell me a secret...

Since ancient times, governments have collected secret information, or *intelligence*, about their enemies – or potential enemies. The people who collect it are known as *spies*, and the work they do is called *espionage*.

What is a spy?

The term 'spy' can mean lots of things.
But it's mainly used to describe someone who gathers secret information about enemy organizations.

This building is the headquarters of SIS, the UK's Secret Intelligence Service, also known as MI6. Find out more on page 10.

Secret agents

Most governments run spy organizations, sometimes known as *agencies*, to gather intelligence and to protect their own secrets. The people who work for them are known as *intelligence agents* or *intelligence officers*.

Agent is sometimes used as another word for *spy*.

Gathering intelligence

- Identifying and handling spies who have access to enemy information. This is called *human intelligence,* or *HUMINT.*
- Monitoring enemy activity and communications. This is known as *technical intelligence (TECHINT),* or *signals intelligence (SIGINT).*
- Examining all intelligence gathered, and assessing it for accuracy and value.

Protecting secrets

- Identifying and expelling enemy spies.
- Keeping internal communications as safe as possible, by using codes, for example.
- Disrupting the work of enemy agencies, known as *counter-espionage.*
- Feeding false information to enemy spies, known as *counter-intelligence.*

Villains or heroes?

Anyone who passes on their country's secrets is a traitor to their home country – but because of the risk involved, they are sometimes regarded as heroes by the country they spy for.

An inside job

A spy who manages to infiltrate a rival organization, or a spy recruited from within an enemy agency, is known as a *mole* – taking their name from the underground animal.

Tailing targets

Spies are often called on to monitor people suspected of being terrorists or enemy spies. These suspects are known as *targets*.

Double agents

Spies who make the enemy believe they are traitors – but are in fact also reporting back to their own spymasters – are called *double agents*.

Deep cover

Some spies live and work for years as ordinary citizens in a foreign country. One day, they may be contacted and given a mission to complete. These agents are known as *sleepers*.

Going underground

Some spies, often known as *field agents,* work undercover. They protect their identities by using a made-up name – their *cover,* or *alias* – and a false life story, known as a *legend.*

Changing faces

If a field agent is recognized, he or she may need to make a quick getaway. Simple tricks, such as wearing a hat or wig, can be enough to help an agent blend in with a crowd, or even fool a security camera.

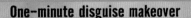

One-minute disguise makeover

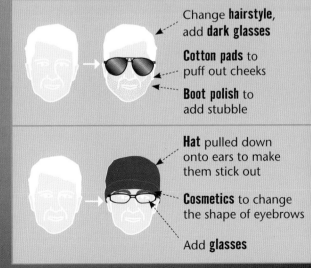

Change **hairstyle,** add **dark glasses**

Cotton pads to puff out cheeks

Boot polish to add stubble

Hat pulled down onto ears to make them stick out

Cosmetics to change the shape of eyebrows

Add **glasses**

Agents in action

There are many branches of espionage. Here are just some of the different tasks that field agents, intelligence officers and analysts might be called upon to do...

Surveillance

This field agent is watching a suspected spy...

...he will follow the suspect to see where he goes and who he talks to.

Stealing secrets

This agent is sneaking onto an enemy's boat...

...hoping to make a copy of a code book that she can pass on to her spymaster.

Exchanging secret messages

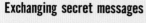

This agent has seen a telltale mark on a drainpipe...

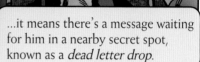

...it means there's a message waiting for him in a nearby secret spot, known as a *dead letter drop.*

Sabotage

An agency has uncovered the location of an enemy weapons factory. They've sent in a team of soldiers to blow it up.

Counter–intelligence

This spy has persuaded an enemy agency that he will sell them secrets. But he's lying...

...he's really a double agent.

Intelligence gathering

This analyst is poring through a dossier relating to a terrorist group...

...If she can crack the coded message, she'll help prevent a terrorist attack. Find out more about codes on page 18.

Spy chart

This chart shows the major intelligence groups in the UK. Most countries run two (or more) agencies, one responsible for gathering intelligence, the other for monitoring threats at home and from overseas.

Government

- All espionage organizations are responsible to the government, ultimately to the Prime Minister.

Joint Intelligence Committee (JIC)

- The chiefs of each organization meet together with a senior minister to discuss new threats, and to decide what new intelligence is needed.

Secret Intelligence Service (MI6)
HQ: Vauxhall Cross, London

Responsible for:
- Discovering threats from foreign countries and helping block them.
- Collecting military and industrial secrets from and in other countries.
- Identifying and recruiting spies within enemy organziations.

Security Service (MI5)
HQ: Thames House, London

Responsible for:
- Seeking out enemies and threats inside the UK.
- Safeguarding military and industrial national secrets.
- Verifying reports of enemy activity gained from spying.

Government Communications Headquarters (GCHQ)
HQ: Cheltenham, UK

Responsible for:
- Collecting, decoding and verifying messages from enemy computers, telephones and other communications sources.

Each agency is made up of *departments* responsible for different tasks. Agents share intelligence between departments and sometimes work together. They can also cooperate with teams from the military and police.

Department A: Communications and technology

- **Technology specialists** plant bugs – hidden microphones – and other surveillance devices at enemy locations. Find out more on pages 14-15.

- **Surveillance officers** monitor the devices, and pass on intelligence to the analysis department.

Department B: Analysis and research

- **Report analysts** use their expert knowledge of science, politics and local conditions.

- **Data analysts** examine satellite photographs and camera images.

- **Language experts and codebreakers** sift through phone calls, emails and other communications. Find out more on pages 20-21.

Department C: In the field

- **Spymasters** and **control officers** find and control spies and defectors.

- **Field agents** infiltrate enemy agencies or terrorist cells, when no internal spies can be found. Find out more on pages 68-69.

- **Combat agents** conduct high-risk operations, such as trailing targets in enemy territory or, in times of war, sabotage missions.

Over the hill

Since ancient times, generals have used spies to observe their enemies. This is known as *reconnaissance* and is still a vital strategy for military forces today.

Airborne spies

Aerial photographs from planes and satellites help agents locate weapons bases and army camps. High-flying UAVs – unmanned airborne vehicles – scour and photograph as much enemy territory as they can.

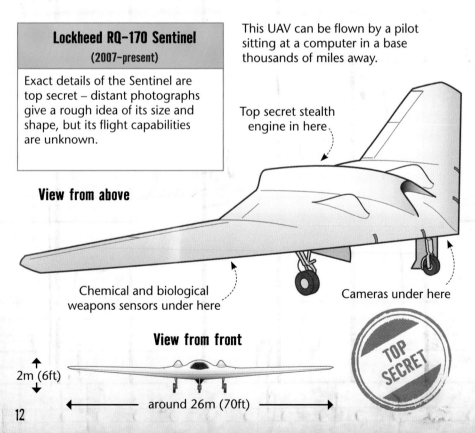

Lockheed RQ-170 Sentinel
(2007–present)

Exact details of the Sentinel are top secret – distant photographs give a rough idea of its size and shape, but its flight capabilities are unknown.

This UAV can be flown by a pilot sitting at a computer in a base thousands of miles away.

View from above

Top secret stealth engine in here

Chemical and biological weapons sensors under here

Cameras under here

View from front

2m (6ft)

around 26m (70ft)

TOP SECRET

The Duke of Wellington, the British general who defeated Napoleon in 1815, said the art of war comes down to 'knowing what's on the other side of the hill'.

This sequence of photographs, taken by British Royal Flying Corps pilots during the First World War (1914-18), shows a set of trenches near the town of Loos, in France.

Intelligence officers joined the photographs together and added labels to identify different trenches.

Spy kit 1: eyes and ears

Spies use an arsenal of machines, robots and hidden weapons to help them on undercover missions. Many of these gadgets are designed for one activity: surveillance.

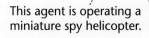

This agent is operating a miniature spy helicopter.

Laser ears

A laser emitter and receiver system allows spies to listen in on conversations through windows.

1. An emitter sends out a laser beam.

2. The beam bounces off the target window and into the receiver.

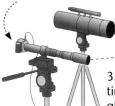

3. The receiver converts tiny movements of the glass into sound.

Bugs

Tiny microphones, known as *bugs*, can be hidden almost anywhere. This bug, inside a light fixture, sends sounds to a spy in a parked van. He or she can listen in to the people talking in the room.

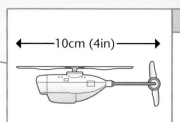

←—10cm (4in)—→

Eyes in the sky

Agents can control miniature helicopters using a laptop. The helicopter follows targets through city streets, sending live pictures and sounds to the agent's computer.

Agencies are sometimes allowed to watch people through police security cameras.

Camera gun

Cameras mounted on top of sniper rifles were developed in the 1950s. They're still used to take long-range photographs.

Not all spying is about gadgets. Sometimes it's simpler just to follow an enemy in person.

Long-range listening

For open-air listening, spies can use large discs called *reflectors*. These can catch and amplify sounds from up to 150m (500ft) away. They can even pick up on a specific conversation across a crowded room or a noisy street.

Secret messages

Spies protect important messages by keeping them hidden. Concealing or disguising information is known as *steganography*. Here are some ingenious examples...

Wax tablet

Over 2,300 years ago, in Ancient Greece, spies scratched messages onto wooden tablets – then covered them over with wax.

They wrote a second, false message on the top layer of wax.

Head space

Another Ancient Greek trick was to write a message on a spy's shaven head. Once his hair grew back, the spy could deliver the message safely.

Even the most suspicious enemies rarely thought to shave a person's head to look for hidden messages.

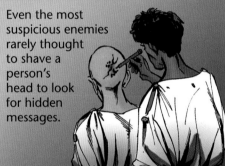

Invisible ink

Certain substances, such as human saliva, milk or juice from citrus fruits, leave a mark that is hard to see in normal light. These are known as *invisible inks*.

Roman generals used this trick nearly 2,000 years ago, and modern versions are still used by spies today.

Many inks can be revealed by warming them gently.

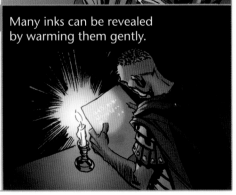

Scout secret

In the late 19th century, British army officer Robert Baden-Powell hid coded pictures inside drawings of butterflies.

First, he drew a small diagram of a foreign fort, showing the position of the guns.

Then, he painted a butterfly around the diagram. Only agents briefed to recognize this trick could see the hidden diagram.

Pixel power

Modern computer files build up pictures using thousands of tiny squares known as pixels. Spies can create a secret message hidden in those pixels.

This image of a butterfly is made up of thousands of pixels using subtly different shades...

...unless you know exactly where to look, you won't spot a small area of pixels that reveals a hidden word or image.

DON'T TRUST

Letters in disguise

For thousands of years, agents have disguised their plans and messages using two different methods to change words: *codes* and *ciphers*.

Codes

A code swaps the true meaning of a message, known as the *plaintext*, for new words, numbers or symbols. Agents make a note of code words in a *codebook* that they only share with friendly agents.

This miniature codebook was used by Russian spies operating in Britain in the 1960s.

The study of codes is called *cryptography*. The art of uncovering hidden messages is known as *cryptanalysis*.

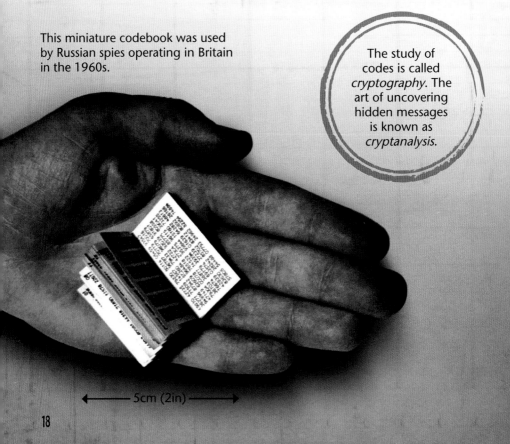

5cm (2in)

Ciphers

Ciphers are more useful for long and complex messages. In a cipher, individual letters of the alphabet are swapped or juggled around. As long as a fellow agent understands how the cipher works, he or she can decode the message.

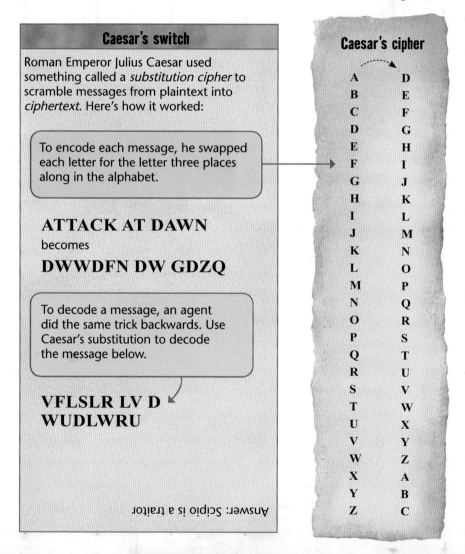

Caesar's switch

Roman Emperor Julius Caesar used something called a *substitution cipher* to scramble messages from plaintext into *ciphertext*. Here's how it worked:

To encode each message, he swapped each letter for the letter three places along in the alphabet.

ATTACK AT DAWN

becomes

DWWDFN DW GDZQ

To decode a message, an agent did the same trick backwards. Use Caesar's substitution to decode the message below.

VFLSLR LV D WUDLWRU

Caesar's cipher

A	D
B	E
C	F
D	G
E	H
F	I
G	J
H	K
I	L
J	M
K	N
L	O
M	P
N	Q
O	R
P	S
Q	T
R	U
S	V
T	W
U	X
V	Y
W	Z
X	A
Y	B
Z	C

Answer: Scipio is a traitor

Secret letter readers

16th-century French king Henry IV set up a team of letter readers and codebreakers to examine suspicious messages.

They were known as the *cabinet noir*, or 'black chamber', after the room where they worked.

This French print from 1816 shows the old king's *cabinet noir* at work reading letters.

Cracking codes

Most codes can only be broken by finding the right codebook, or by persuading a captured spy to explain it. For centuries, torture was used as a means of persuasion – but it wasn't very reliable.

This 16th-century print shows a man being tortured on a device called a rack.

Solving ciphers

Deciphering means translating a ciphertext message into plaintext. Analysts can sometimes crack ciphers even without a codebook, using a variety of mathematical and linguistic tricks.

Cipher secrets

Ciphers have a weakness – common letters. All languages have some letters that are used more often than others. If a codebreaker can find these, it helps them start deciphering.

Look at this cipher message: *p dpss tlla fvb ha aol zlhzpkl*

P dpss tlla

fvb ha aol

zlhzpkl

L appears five times.

The codebreaker starts by assuming the cipher is based on the English alphabet. In English, the letter 'e' appears most, followed by 't' and 'a'.

A = H
B = I
C = J
D = K
E = L
F = M
G = N
H = O
I = P
J = Q

The most common letter in the cipher is likely to correspond to the most common letter in the original language. Here, 'l' corresponds to 'e'.

The codebreaker then tries a number of well-known ciphers, such as the 'Caesar substitution' cipher described on page 19.

P DPSS TLLA FVB HA AOL ZLHZPKL
I WILL MEET YOU AT THE SEASIDE

Spies of the ancient world

Spying is often described as one of the world's oldest professions. Over 2,500 years ago, Chinese general Sun Tzu included an entire chapter on spy tactics in his manual *The Art of War*.

Spartan scytales

Around 2,300 years ago, Spartan generals used rods called *scytales* to compose and decipher secret messages hidden on leather belts.

False letters disguise the message.

2. A messenger unwound the belt and carried it to General Y.

1. General X looped a belt around a scytale and wrote the message across the loops.

3. General Y wrapped the belt around his own scytale. The scytale had to be the same width as General X's to reveal the original message.

Hannibal's handshakes

A little over 2,000 years ago, Carthaginian general Hannibal used spies to infiltrate Roman legions, so he could learn their plans and ambush them.

Hannibal's spies used secret handshakes to identify themselves to each other – the oldest known use of this trick.

Assassins

11th-century Persian leader Hassan-i-Sabbah founded a cult of elite warriors. Their enemies named these fearsome opponents *Hashashin*.

Sabbah sent his warriors to murder his enemies in secret – a type of mission now known as *assassination*.

Ninjas

In 15th-century Japan, rival warlords used spies-for-hire known as *ninjas*.

Legends claimed ninjas could turn invisible and walk on water.

Ninjas dressed in dark blue to hide in the shadows.

Pochteca

15th-century Aztec chiefs hired merchants known as *pochteca* to gather intelligence about enemy towns.

Pochteca traded important wares all over Central and South America, giving them access to enemy strongholds.

Lord of the spies

Queen Elizabeth I of England relied on a brilliant spymaster, Sir Francis Walsingham, to protect her crown and country. Walsingham hired a network of spies, known as *intelligencers*, to infiltrate groups of potential plotters.

Storm warnings

In 1588, Walsingham's agents discovered that the King of Spain was sending a fleet, the *Armada*, to invade England. Elizabeth's admirals had enough warning to prepare.

The Babington plot

In 1586, Walsingham's intelligencers intercepted a message from Mary, Queen of Scots, to a courtier named Anthony Babington.

By deciphering the message, they uncovered an attempt to assassinate Elizabeth, and place Mary on the throne. Babington and Mary were both executed.

Mary's nomenclator

Mary scrambled her messages by combining a cipher with a set of code words, a trick known as a *nomenclator*.

Can you translate this message?

This 18th century painting shows the British fleet intercepting and defeating the *Armada* using fire ships.

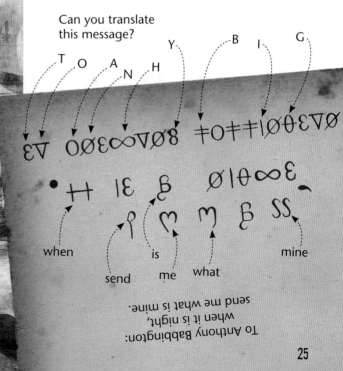

To Anthony Babbington:
when it is night,
send me what is mine.

Spy detectives

In 1850, American businessman Allan Pinkerton founded one of the world's first private detective agencies – the Pinkertons.

The Pinkertons were hired by government agencies to help fight crime all over the USA.

The motto used by Pinkerton to promote his agency was "We never sleep."

One of the gang

Pinkerton agents were sometimes called in to infiltrate a criminal gang. They lived under a cover identity for months at a time, reporting to spymasters in secret.

Allan Pinkerton, top left, with a team of his agents

Rogues gallery

Pinkerton created a database of known and suspected criminals. Upon arrest, he added fingerprints, photographs and other details. Secret services still use this kind of database to help identify spies.

This Pinkerton Agency file features George Parker and Harry Longbaugh, better known as the bank robbers *Butch Cassidy* and *the Sundance Kid*.

The information supplied by the Pinkertons led to the capture of several members of Parker's gang – the *Wild Bunch*.

First photo taken July 1894

Name George Parker, alias *Butch Cassidy*, alias *George Cassidy*, alias *Ingerfield*

Last photo taken Nov. 1900

Name Harry Longbaugh, alias *Kid Longbaugh*, alias *Harry Alonzo*, alias *Frank Jones*, alias *Frank Boyd*, alias *the Sundance Kid*.

Intelligence on tap

From 1861-1865, the northern Unionist states and southern Confederate states of the USA were divided by civil war. Both sides used spies, and a new invention – the telegraph – to improve their chances of victory.

Down the wire

Soldiers used telegraph wires to send instant messages to their commanders miles away. Spies learned how to listen in to, or *tap*, these messages by hooking up a portable receiver.

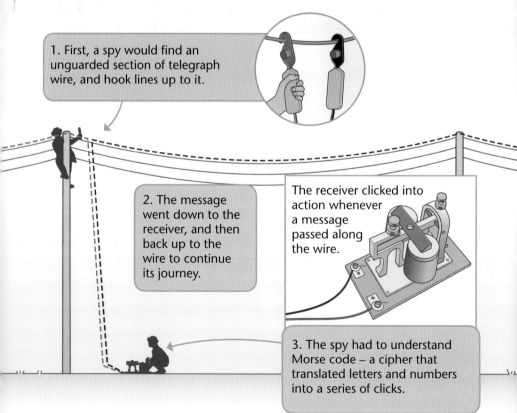

1. First, a spy would find an unguarded section of telegraph wire, and hook lines up to it.

2. The message went down to the receiver, and then back up to the wire to continue its journey.

The receiver clicked into action whenever a message passed along the wire.

3. The spy had to understand Morse code – a cipher that translated letters and numbers into a series of clicks.

Real spies No. 1: the society lady

Name: Belle Boyd

Spymaster: Confederate army Colonel Turner Ashby

Background: Early in the War, Boyd's house was under armed guard by Unionist soldiers.

Spy mission: Boyd charmed the guards and learned military secrets from them. She sent one of her slaves, Eliza Hopewell, to pass on these secrets to her spymaster.

Exposed: Boyd's tricks were discovered by a guard. In 1862 she was arrested and imprisoned.

ARRESTED

Real spies No. 2: the scout

NEVER CAUGHT

Name: Harriet Tubman

Spymaster: Union army General David Hunter

Background: Tubman, who had escaped slavery before the Civil War broke out, spent many years helping other slaves escape to the northern USA.

Spy mission: To pass unseen through enemy territory, bringing back maps and other vital intelligence from the southern states.

Spies at war

Spies, saboteurs and codebreakers played a key part in every stage of the First World War – a conflict that involved countries around the globe from 1914 to 1918.

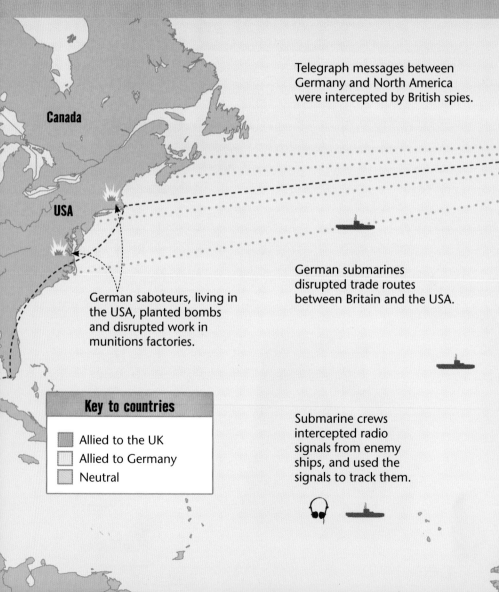

Telegraph messages between Germany and North America were intercepted by British spies.

Canada

USA

German saboteurs, living in the USA, planted bombs and disrupted work in munitions factories.

German submarines disrupted trade routes between Britain and the USA.

Key to countries

Allied to the UK
Allied to Germany
Neutral

Submarine crews intercepted radio signals from enemy ships, and used the signals to track them.

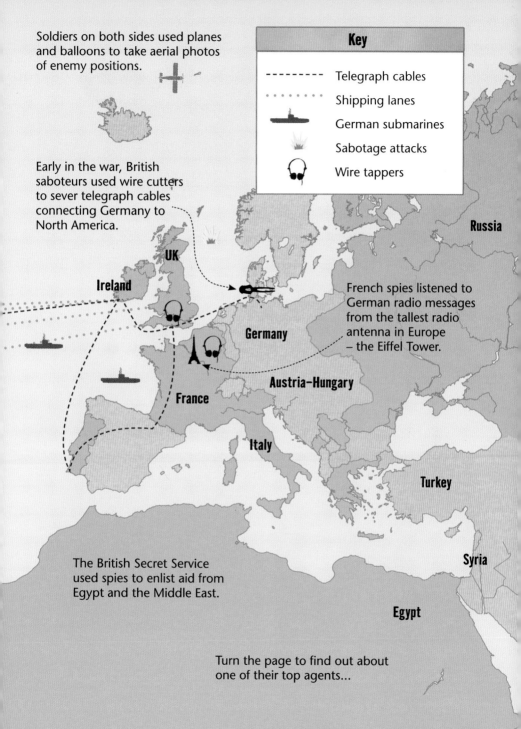

Soldiers on both sides used planes and balloons to take aerial photos of enemy positions.

Key

------------ Telegraph cables

.... Shipping lanes

German submarines

Sabotage attacks

Wire tappers

Early in the war, British saboteurs used wire cutters to sever telegraph cables connecting Germany to North America.

Russia

UK

Ireland

French spies listened to German radio messages from the tallest radio antenna in Europe – the Eiffel Tower.

Germany

Austria–Hungary

France

Italy

Turkey

The British Secret Service used spies to enlist aid from Egypt and the Middle East.

Syria

Egypt

Turn the page to find out about one of their top agents...

31

The desert spy

DATE: 1916-1918

LOCATION: The deserts of the Middle East

BACKGROUND: The Turkish army occupied Syria and the deserts east of the Red Sea. The British were at war with the Turks, but knew they couldn't succeed without help from the Arabs who lived there.

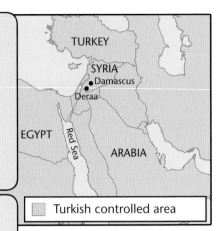

Turkish controlled area

THE MISSION: British Intelligence sent a young soldier named T. E. Lawrence to enlist the aid of the Bedouin – nomadic Arab tribes who lived in the desert.

Lawrence was fluent in Arabic and understood the customs of the Bedouin. He dressed and lived as one of them, and impressed their leaders with his endurance on long camel rides across endless deserts.

During his mission, Lawrence was captured by Turkish agents while scouting in the town of Deraa.

He survived a brutal interrogation, and convinced his captors he was Georgian and not British. He was left tied up in a store cupboard, but managed to escape.

Lawrence persuaded Bedouin chiefs not to fight the Turkish army openly, but to use sabotage and raiding tactics on their supply trains.

Camel raiders

Turkish supply train

He called in help from the British army to provide fortified cars and even fighter planes to help the Bedouin raid Turkish forts.

Machine gun

Bristol fighter

Metal-plated Rolls-Royce

Turkish fort

By October 1918, the Arabs had taken control of the key city of Damascus, and the Turks soon asked for a ceasefire.

TURKEY

SYRIA

• Damascus

Lawrence wrote about his exploits, and became one of Britain's most famous spy heroes: Lawrence of Arabia.

The Zimmermann telegram

In January 1917, British codebreakers at Room 40 – a black chamber unit at British Royal Navy headquarters in London – intercepted a suspicious-looking German telegram intended for the Mexican government.

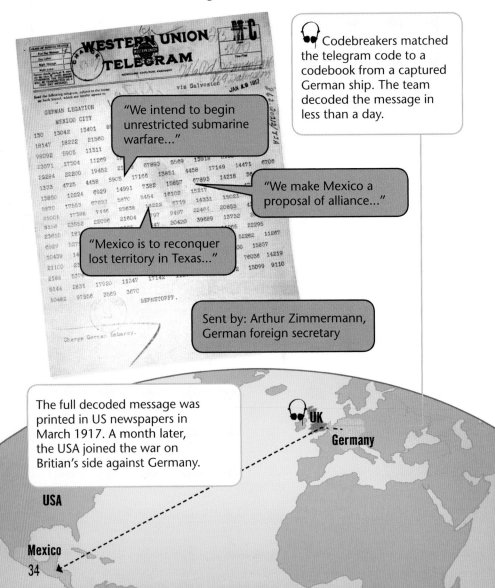

Codebreakers matched the telegram code to a codebook from a captured German ship. The team decoded the message in less than a day.

"We intend to begin unrestricted submarine warfare..."

"We make Mexico a proposal of alliance..."

"Mexico is to reconquer lost territory in Texas..."

Sent by: Arthur Zimmermann, German foreign secretary

The full decoded message was printed in US newspapers in March 1917. A month later, the USA joined the war on Britian's side against Germany.

USA

Mexico

UK

Germany

Real spies No. 3: the celebrity

Real name: Margaretha Zelle

Codename: *H-21*

Spymasters: German officers across Europe

Background: Zelle was a dancer who found fame in 1905 under the stage name *Mata Hari*. Her dance act was inspired by years spent living in the Dutch East Indies (modern-day Indonesia). It made her a celebrity in Paris and other European cities.

Spy mission: Zelle was invited to parties to meet many leading French generals and politicians. Her German spymasters paid her to cajole secrets from them.

Exposed: French spies intercepted German radio messages describing a spy codenamed *H-21*, who could only be the famous dancer.

Trial: Zelle was arrested in Paris in February 1917. The main evidence against her was that invisible ink was found in her cosmetics bag.

Final fate: executed by firing squad in October 1917.

Global espionage

The First World War brought huge changes. A new regime, the Soviet Union, replaced the old Russian empire. It began to recruit an army of spies to run missions across the world.

Secret police

The Soviet government enforced its rule through a ruthless secret police force eventually named the NKVD, the Russian initials for the 'People's Comissariat for Internal Affairs'.

A new name

In the 1950s, the NKVD was replaced by a new and even more feared spy organization, the 'Committee for State Security', or KGB.

The Lubyanka Building in Moscow has been the headquarters of many Russian spy agencies, including the NKVD and the KGB.

A bigger bureau

The American FBI – Federal Bureau of Investigation – had been set up in 1908 to fight criminals within the USA. With the rise of Soviet spy agencies, the FBI expanded to help combat the threat of enemy agents working in the USA.

Reds under the bed

Soviet spies, and Soviet sympathizers, were known as *Reds* in America – because of the Soviet Union's bright, red flag. Throughout the 1920s and 1930s, NKVD and KGB teams set up spy rings across the USA.

FBI agents often trailed suspects, including 'Reds', hidden inside plain-looking cars.

The Second World War

By 1940, Nazi Germany had successfully invaded much of Western Europe. A new breed of spies emerged – *resistance* fighters, who worked against the Germans from inside countries including France, Norway, Belgium and the Netherlands.

Special Ops

The UK, still unoccupied, assisted resistance groups by sending in field agents to collect intelligence and help with sabotage missions. This organization was known as the SOE (Special Operations Executive).

The SOE was the first branch of the military to recruit and train women for field work.

SOE agent disguised as French Resistance fighter.

Sten machine gun

Suppressor to muffle the sound and hide the flash of shots

SOE agents learned how to send and receive messages using portable radios.

SOE agent (UK, 1940-1946)

Main missions:
- Passing messages
- Gathering information
- Smuggling weapons to resistance groups

The Cretan kidnap

DATE: April 1944

LOCATION: Crete

SITUATION: The German army had captured the Greek island of Crete in 1941. Local resistance fighters were locked in a brutal struggle against the Germans, with occasional help from the SOE.

GREECE

TURKEY

CRETE

Mediterranean Sea

EGYPT

THE MISSION: In 1944, two SOE officers, W. Stanley Moss and Patrick Leigh Fermor, planned to kidnap the latest German general in charge of Crete.

Moss and Fermor disguised themselves as German military policeman, and waited on a quiet road.

That night, they captured the general at gunpoint.

Cretan resistance fighters helped the kidnappers and their captive hide in caves. They moved at night, out of sight of German patrols.

12 days later, the agents were able to smuggle the general onto a Royal Navy ship. The mission was a success.

Spy kit 2: SOE gadgets

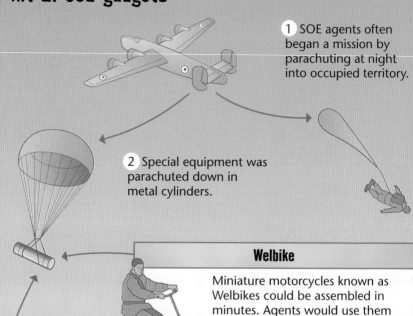

1 SOE agents often began a mission by parachuting at night into occupied territory.

2 Special equipment was parachuted down in metal cylinders.

Welbike

Miniature motorcycles known as Welbikes could be assembled in minutes. Agents would use them to ride from an isolated drop zone into position near a town.

Welrod pistol

Barrel   Stock

Welrod pistols had a stock that could be detached from the barrel, allowing an agent to hide two tubes inside a long coat.

Wireless experts

Some SOE agents carried simple electrical equipment, and even instruction manuals on how to build radio transmitters to send messages back home.

Night drops

In the summer of 1940, British SOE agents began to slip into regions occupied by their enemies, both in Europe and in the Far East. They carried lightweight, disguised equipment and weapons, to help them blend in with the local population.

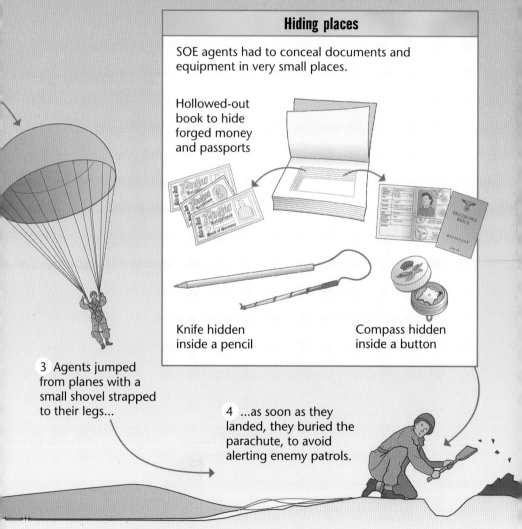

Hiding places

SOE agents had to conceal documents and equipment in very small places.

Hollowed-out book to hide forged money and passports

Knife hidden inside a pencil

Compass hidden inside a button

3 Agents jumped from planes with a small shovel strapped to their legs...

4 ...as soon as they landed, they buried the parachute, to avoid alerting enemy patrols.

Secret languages

Radio signals allowed generals to bring together troops, field guns and fighter planes in massive, joined-up attacks. Spies struggled to create the best codes: easy to use, but impossible to crack for anyone listening in.

Code talkers

US Marines employed Native American Navajo volunteers to develop a code based on their language. For example, submarines were called *béésh tóó*, which is Navajo for 'iron fish'.

Enemy spies never broke the Navajo code. It was used by the US Army until the 1970s.

Navajo volunteers became radio operators, translating messages into Navajo and then using a code.

Code machines

By the start of the War, most countries' military teams used devices called cryptography machines to convert messages into ciphertext. The text could only be deciphered by someone using the same machine, set to the correct settings.

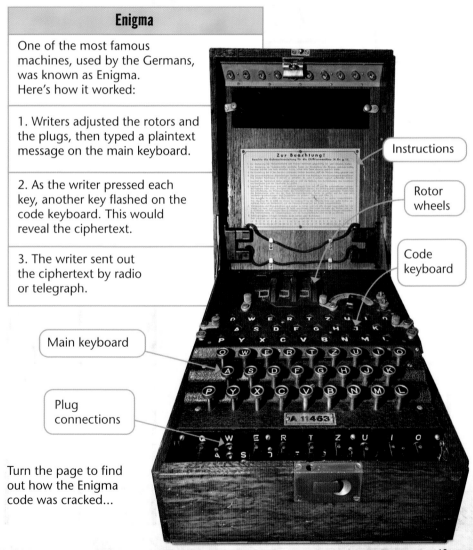

Enigma

One of the most famous machines, used by the Germans, was known as Enigma. Here's how it worked:

1. Writers adjusted the rotors and the plugs, then typed a plaintext message on the main keyboard.

2. As the writer pressed each key, another key flashed on the code keyboard. This would reveal the ciphertext.

3. The writer sent out the ciphertext by radio or telegraph.

Instructions

Rotor wheels

Code keyboard

Main keyboard

Plug connections

A 11463

Turn the page to find out how the Enigma code was cracked...

Codebreakers

During the War, intelligence agencies employed large teams of experts, such as mathematicians, to crack machine codes. The most successful was based at Bletchley Park, Berkshire, UK. They worked in secrecy to unlock the Enigma code, but they'd never have succeeded without the help of dedicated spies...

Cracking Enigma

1931 A French mole in Germany passed on photos of an early Enigma manual.

1936 Polish codebreakers used the manual to construct an Enigma machine, allowing them to decipher messages.

1939 The Germans added extra sets of rotors to their machines, making the code harder to break.

Teams of analysts in Bletchley Park worked around the clock to translate new messages picked up over the radio.

Computer crackers

The Bletchley Park team built the world's first digital computers.

These vast machines were able to process thousands of different settings on machines, such as Enigma, to try to unscramble messages.

1941 British field agents recovered two new Enigma machines from a German ship.

1942 Using a new computer, the team at Bletchley Park were able to decipher German messages.

Decoded messages were classified above top secret, given the codename *Ultra*.

ULTRA

Mind games

While spies collect and steal secrets, they also go to incredible
lengths to feed misleading information to enemy agents.

Misinformation

Early in the War, the Germans recruited a British criminal named
Eddie Chapman as a spy and saboteur. Chapman adopted the
codename *Fritz*. But soon after beginning his mission, he offered
himself to MI5 as a British double agent, codenamed *Zigzag*...

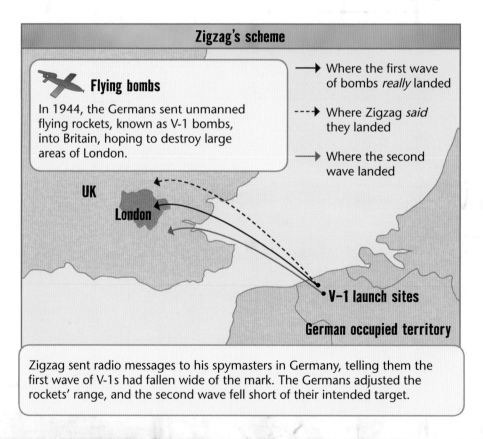

Zigzag's scheme

Flying bombs

In 1944, the Germans sent unmanned
flying rockets, known as V-1 bombs,
into Britain, hoping to destroy large
areas of London.

→ Where the first wave
of bombs *really* landed

--→ Where Zigzag *said*
they landed

→ Where the second
wave landed

UK

London

• V-1 launch sites

German occupied territory

Zigzag sent radio messages to his spymasters in Germany, telling them the
first wave of V-1s had fallen wide of the mark. The Germans adjusted the
rockets' range, and the second wave fell short of their intended target.

Fatal deception

In the Spring of 1943, the Allies were poised to invade the island of Sicily. A Royal Navy intelligence team devised a plan to convince the Germans that they were *really* going to attack Greece. The plan was called *Operation Mincemeat.*

A combined intelligence team disguised a corpse as a Royal Marine major, and dropped it in the sea near Spain. They made it look as if there had been a plane crash.

Fishermen found the body and handed it over to the Spanish army, who passed it over to the Germans...

...along with a briefcase containing fake plans for an invasion of Greece.

Officers also found the Major's wallet, along with unpaid bills, bus tickets, even love letters from his fiancée. All had been carefully planted to create a believable identity.

The legend was so convincing that the fake plans ended up being sent to the German leader, Adolf Hitler.

He ordered troops away from Sicily and into Greece...

...so the British scheme was a success.

Old friends, new enemies

The USA and the Soviet Union had fought as allies in the Second World War. But, with different political outlooks, these superpowers soon became bitter enemies in a conflict known as the Cold War. This time, spies were on the front line...

Spy vs. spy

Spies on both sides were desperate to learn about each other's military strength. Espionage missions between the rival superpowers and their allies continued for almost 40 years.

Nuclear secrets

By 1949, both superpowers had developed their own versions of an apocalyptic new weapon – the atomic bomb. This nuclear-powered explosive had the power to destroy whole cities.

The US tested their bombs at sea – unaware that Soviet spy ships disguised as fishing boats were often watching from a distance.

The US government tested many atomic bombs near the Marshall Islands in the Pacific Ocean.

Real spies No. 4: the scientist

Real name: Klaus Fuchs

Codename: *REST*

Spymasters: Soviet Union

Background: German-born physicist Fuchs had fled the Nazi regime before the War and moved to the USA. He was part of the team that built the first working nuclear bombs.

Spy mission: Soon after the War, Fuchs supplied Soviet scientists with information to help them build their own nuclear weapons, and let them know how well-armed the US was.

Exposed: British and US agencies cracked a Soviet code known as *Venona* in 1946. Fuchs was identified as a spy, codename *REST*.

Captured: Fuchs, now living in Britain, was questioned by MI5, and eventually arrested in 1951.

Final fate: Fuchs served nine years of a 14-year prison sentence. He moved to East Germany after his release, his days as a spy now behind him.

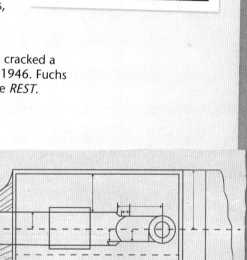

This is part of a sketch that Fuchs passed to his spymaster in 1948, showing a plan for a hydrogen bomb – an atomic weapon.

East vs. West

One hotspot in the Cold War was Berlin, a city deep inside Soviet-controlled East Germany. After the War, the city had been split between the victorious armies.
A barbed-wire fence isolated non-Soviet West Berlin from the Soviet-controlled Eastern sector of the city.

Western agents often worked together to spy on the Soviets in the East.

In 1961, the East Germans built a brick wall that surrounded almost the whole of West Berlin.

French Sector

British Sector

WEST BERLIN

American Sector

EAST BERLIN
(under Soviet control)

Secret tunnel

In 1952, a British mole in the KGB passed on the location of Soviet phone cables near the East-West divide. Working together, the CIA and MI6 dug a tunnel and tapped into those cables.

CIA office, disguised as a warehouse

Barbed wire fence, put up in the decade before the main wall

West Berlin side

Shaft connecting warehouse to tunnel

5m (16ft) deep

Sandbags along the tunnel wall helped muffle the sound of footsteps and voices.

450m (500 yards)

East German police kept a constant watch along the Wall. They reported any suspicious activity to a ruthless secret police organization known as the *Stasi*.

RLINER GEHT MIT ┬ POLITISCHE KAMPFANSAGE ┬ SUCH
R AUF DIE MAUER AM GEGEN DIE MILITARISCHE ┃ GESE
AUTORITAT UND

The Soviets knew about the tunnel before it was even built, from an MI6 mole. Instead of shutting it down, they kept quiet until 1956 – helping to protect the identity of their mole.

East Berlin side

Locked steel door to protect agents from capture

Underground phone cables

Railway system to transport equipment

Recording chamber

Tap chamber

Circles of deceit

Some agents dedicate years of their life to a false identity.
If they can successfully enter a foreign country, they can
set up a *spy ring* to provide a flow of secrets.

How a spy ring works

Control The agent who sets up the spy ring is sometimes known as a *control officer*. He or she will identify someone who works for a government agency, and try to recruit them as a spy.

Control officers sometimes use bribes or blackmail to get spies to work for them.

The spy, now known as **Agent A,** recruits other spies to help gather secrets.

Control and Agent A communicate using a dead letter drop (see page 9). They avoid meeting in person.

Drop point

Dead drop signal

Agent A collects all the intelligence from **Agents B, C** and **D** and passes it along to Control.

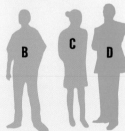

Agent A does not reveal Control's identity – so even if Agents B, C or D are exposed, they cannot tell the enemy who Control is.

Real spies No. 5: the third man

Real name: Harold 'Kim' Philby

Codenames: *Synok*; *Agent Stanley*

Nationality: British

Spymasters: NKVD and KGB

ESCAPED

Background: Philby joined the SOE during the Second World War, and afterwards became a high-ranking officer in MI6.

Spy mission: Long before the War, Philby had been recruited by a Soviet control officer, known by the codename *Mar*. Philby passed secrets to *Mar* for many years.

Exposed: In 1945, MI6 found out that secrets were being leaked to the Soviet Union. Philby himself was involved in the investigation that exposed two spies, only to find himself accused of being the 'third man' in a spy ring. Philby resigned from MI6 in 1952, and was cleared of being a spy by 1955.

Final fate: In 1961, a Soviet defector revealed that Philby was, in fact, Agent A in a five-man spy ring.

Philby, along with two other members of the ring, escaped to live the rest of his life in the Soviet Union. He was given the title 'Hero of the Soviet Union'.

Philby in Moscow in 1968

CIA around the world

America's CIA (Central Intelligence Agency), created in 1947, is still one of the giants of world espionage. This map shows just a few examples of past CIA spy activity across the globe.

Central Intelligence Agency (CIA)
HQ: Langley, Virginia, USA

Responsible for:
- Discovering threats from foreign countries and blocking them.
- Identifying and following enemies around the world.
- Monitoring suspicious activity at home and abroad.

Central America (1960s and 1970s)

Supporting US-friendly governments against rebel groups.

Cuba (1961)

Secret missions to try to remove the Soviet-friendly Cuban regime.

Berlin (1947)

Keeping track of changes in Soviet military strength in East Germany.

Iraq (1990s)

Surveillance work during the Gulf War.

Iran (1953)

Covert missions to try to change the Iranian government, in order to promote US interests.

Korea (1950)

Intelligence gathering missions in North Korea and China.

Angola (1975)

Supporting invasion with the goal of removing its pro-Soviet government.

Pakistan (2011)

Intelligence work leading to the discovery of terrorist leader Osama bin Laden. (Find out more on page 68.)

Vietnam (1960s)

Intelligence gathering in the build-up to and during the Vietnam War.

Eyes in the sky

During the Cold War, the CIA's main task was to watch for threats from the Soviet Union. After unsuccessful attempts to plant moles in the KGB, the CIA took to the skies...

Weather balloons

In the 1950s, the CIA sent high-altitude balloons drifting above parts of the Soviet Union. Each balloon carried a powerful camera.

These balloons were disguised as weather-recording instruments.

Camera in here

The space age

In 1959, the CIA launched its first spy satellite into orbit around the Earth. Pictures taken by a camera on board were dropped in a capsule attached to a parachute.

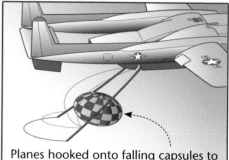

Planes hooked onto falling capsules to collect information from satellites.

Spy planes

Spy planes, such as the Lockheed U-2, allowed the CIA to photograph precise locations in amazing detail. The very existence of the U-2 plane was a CIA secret during the 1950s.

The Cuban missile crisis

In October 1962, a U-2 pilot photographed a missile base in Cuba, an island off the coast of the USA that had close links to the Soviet Union. CIA analysts were sure the bases in the photographs were ready for nuclear missiles.

Missile launch platform

Missile shelter

Missile transporters

Missile fuel oxidizer tanks

Fuel tanks

For a short period, the world seemed to be on the brink of nuclear war. After 13 days of threats and talks, the Soviet government agreed to remove its missiles from Cuba. US spy planes verified this action, and the crisis was over.

Captured!

Field agents can expect a tough reception if they get caught on a mission. But few are killed immediately – they are more likely to be interrogated or, in some cases, tortured.

Tough choices

Spies are trained to stick to their cover story. In wartime, some agents even carry hidden poison pills so they can kill themselves to avoid betraying secrets. Others smuggle escape kits into prison and try to break free.

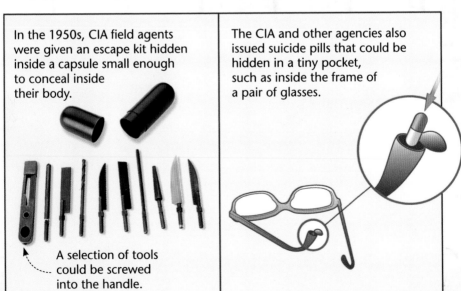

In the 1950s, CIA field agents were given an escape kit hidden inside a capsule small enough to conceal inside their body.

A selection of tools could be screwed into the handle.

The CIA and other agencies also issued suicide pills that could be hidden in a tiny pocket, such as inside the frame of a pair of glasses.

Real spies No. 6: the pilot

CAPTURED

Real name: Gary Powers

Occupation: US Air Force pilot

Spymasters: CIA

Background: Powers was a U-2 spy plane pilot. At the time, these planes were so secret that the US government denied they existed.

Spy mission: In May 1960, Powers was shot down while flying over Russia, hoping to photograph missile bases.

He parachuted to the ground, only to be captured by the KGB. They also recovered vital parts of the plane, including the camera.

Final fate: After months of brutal interrogation, Powers was put on trial, and locked away in a Soviet prison for the crime of spying.

In February 1962, he was taken to a bridge in Berlin, where he was exchanged for a KGB spy who had been arrested by America's FBI.

Powers returned to the USA and worked as a test pilot for Lockheed, the company who built the U-2.

This photo shows Soviet troops and civilians looking at the wreckage of the U-2 plane flown by Powers.

Spy kit 3: gadgets in disguise

Field agents try to keep their true identity hidden by using weapons and other tools disguised as harmless objects.

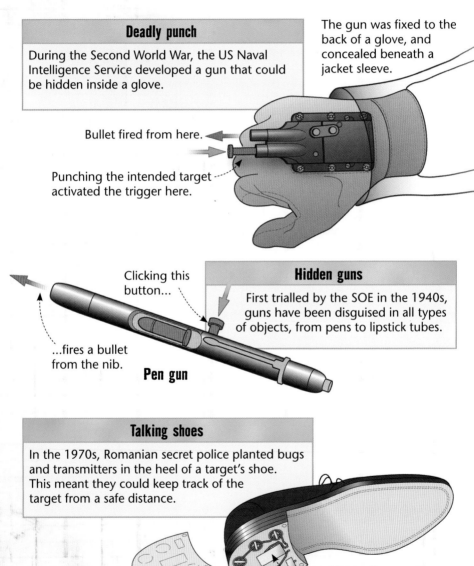

Deadly punch

During the Second World War, the US Naval Intelligence Service developed a gun that could be hidden inside a glove.

The gun was fixed to the back of a glove, and concealed beneath a jacket sleeve.

Bullet fired from here. ◀

Punching the intended target activated the trigger here.

Clicking this button...

...fires a bullet from the nib.

Pen gun

Hidden guns

First trialled by the SOE in the 1940s, guns have been disguised in all types of objects, from pens to lipstick tubes.

Talking shoes

In the 1970s, Romanian secret police planted bugs and transmitters in the heel of a target's shoe. This meant they could keep track of the target from a safe distance.

Hidden bug and transmitter

60

Real spies No. 7: the assassin

Prime suspect: Francesco Gullino or Giullino

Codename: *Piccadilly*

Nationality: Danish/Italian

Base of operations: Europe

Occupation: Alleged assassin

Spymasters: Bulgarian secret police, possibly also the KGB.

AT LARGE

Background: An ex-smuggler who operated all over Europe, recruited by the Bulgarian Secret Service to undertake deadly missions in the West.

Alleged victim: Georgi Markov, a Bulgarian journalist living in London, who had voiced strong anti-Soviet sentiments. Markov was killed by an assassin, probably Gullino, at a bus stop.

Final fate: Gullino admitted to spying for the Bulgarian government. But so far, not enough hard evidence has been found to prove once and for all that he ever worked as an assassin.

Deadly umbrella

Markov's killer used an umbrella that hid a small pellet tipped with ricin – a deadly poison.

Pressing a stud here caused the pellet to shoot out with enough force to stab a person.

Robot spies

Unmanned vehicles, known as *drones*, can be used for all sorts of surveillance missions. With no drivers or pilots, they're smaller – and harder to detect – than manned spy vehicles.

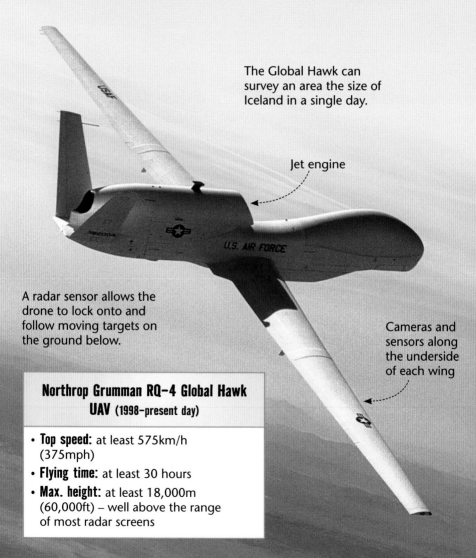

The Global Hawk can survey an area the size of Iceland in a single day.

Jet engine

A radar sensor allows the drone to lock onto and follow moving targets on the ground below.

Cameras and sensors along the underside of each wing

Northrop Grumman RQ–4 Global Hawk UAV (1998–present day)

- **Top speed:** at least 575km/h (375mph)
- **Flying time:** at least 30 hours
- **Max. height:** at least 18,000m (60,000ft) – well above the range of most radar screens

Underwater secrets

Drone submersibles, known as UUVs (Unmanned Underwater Vehicles), can be adapted for spying, surveillance and even military operations.

Kongsberg C'inspector UUV
(2010–present day)

- **Length:** 1.6m (5ft 3in)
- **Mission time:** At least 2 hours
- **Max. depth:** At least 300m (800ft)

This UUV is connected to its operating cable by a micro-thin cable, which extends more than 4km (2 miles).

Propulsion unit

This tiny UUV is designed for coastal patrol, to identify threats on the sea bed and to investigate suspicious ships.

It can be fitted with sensors to detect bombs, chemical weapons, enemy UUVs and more.

Many spy vehicles have been developed by a US agency known as DARPA: Defense Advanced Research Projects Agency.

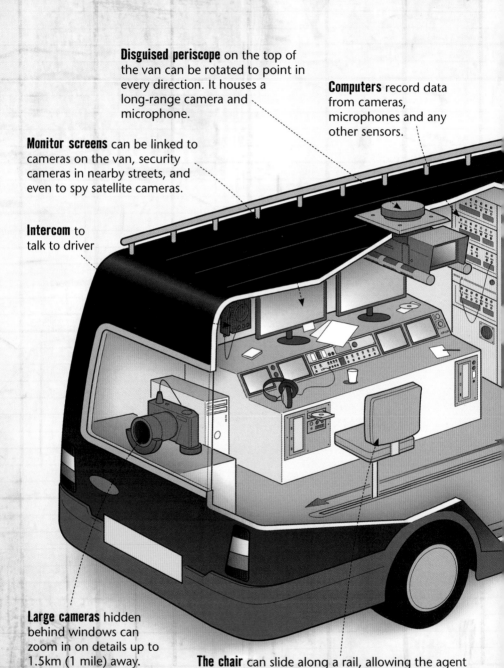

Disguised periscope on the top of the van can be rotated to point in every direction. It houses a long-range camera and microphone.

Computers record data from cameras, microphones and any other sensors.

Monitor screens can be linked to cameras on the van, security cameras in nearby streets, and even to spy satellite cameras.

Intercom to talk to driver

Large cameras hidden behind windows can zoom in on details up to 1.5km (1 mile) away.

The chair can slide along a rail, allowing the agent to move between different controls quickly.

Spy kit 4: surveillance van

A small spy team can run long-term missions from the comfort and secrecy of an ordinary-looking van. On the inside, spy vans can be filled with all sorts of high-tech gear...

Toilet cubicle allows an agent to stay inside for days at a time.

Locked steel door to protect driver's compartment

Tinted windows make it difficult for people to see inside the van.

Cameras and microphones are hidden inside headlights, side lights and rear brake lights.

Carpets and foam insulation keep the van silent, and help keep agents inside warm.

When parked for a long mission, spies can connect power cables to the main electricity supply in the street below.

For long range work, surveillance teams can access satellites in space. These can zoom in close enough to read street names.

Behind enemy lines

Getting to a mission location in enemy territory is known as *insertion*. Field agents sometimes use special equipment to get in and out of hard-to-reach locations.

Martin Jetpack (2008–present day)

- **Top speed:** 110km/h (60mph)
- **Flying time:** 30 minutes
- **Max. height:** 1,500m (5,000ft)

Fans behind each shoulder lift the pilot into the air.

Despite its name, the Martin Jetpack is powered by fans rather than jets. It is really a 'backpack helicopter'.

It can reach landing points that are too tight or dangerous for even the smallest manned helicopters.

Flaps behind the pilot's feet control the flight direction and height.

Balloon escape

Getting out of a danger zone is called *extraction*. In the 1950s, CIA inventor Robert Fulton developed a mechanism he named *Skyhook*, a package that could be dropped down to an agent who has called for extraction from a remote area.

How Skyhook worked

1. The agent puts on a harness, then inflates a bright balloon with helium gas.

Gas canister

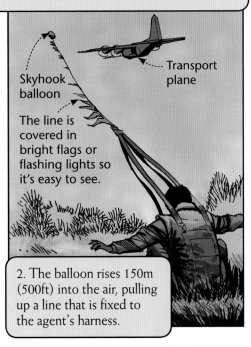

Transport plane

Skyhook balloon

The line is covered in bright flags or flashing lights so it's easy to see.

2. The balloon rises 150m (500ft) into the air, pulling up a line that is fixed to the agent's harness.

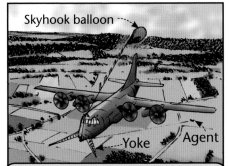

Skyhook balloon

Yoke

Agent

3. A transport plane finds the balloon and catches the line on a wide net called a yoke. The line and agent are whisked under the plane.

Entrance hatch

4. The plane's crew catch the line using a long hook, then winch the agent to safety on board.

Countering terrorism

Intelligence agents use every resource available to monitor terrorist groups, in the hope of catching ringleaders.

Manhunt: Osama bin Laden
The CIA spent over a decade hunting international terrorist Osama bin Laden, using a host of different spy tactics to find and – ultimately – kill him.
• **2007** Intensive interrogation of several known associates of bin Laden revealed the true identity of one of his most trusted companions.
• **May 2010** Combining phone taps and stalking tactics, the CIA followed the companion to a compound in Pakistan. But who lived inside?
• **2010–2011** With the help of satellites and spy planes, the CIA was able to draw up a detailed map of the compound.
• **May 2nd 2011** The US President ordered a Special Forces team to storm the compound. During the fighting, bin Laden was shot and killed.

Local spies watched the compound from a nearby building.

The combined intelligence suggested that bin Laden himself was living in the main house.

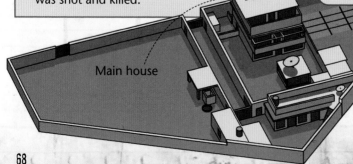

Main house

Spy soldiers

The ultimate field agents, known as Special Forces, work for military agencies. They use the latest weapons and vehicles designed for stealth and combat missions.

Black Hawk

The raid on bin Laden's compound was carried out by US Navy SEAL Team Six, using Black Hawk helicopters.

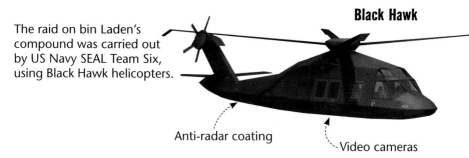

Anti-radar coating

Video cameras

US Special Forces soldiers with combat gear

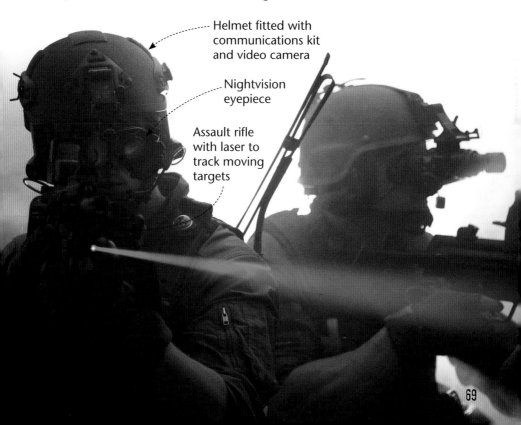

Helmet fitted with communications kit and video camera

Nightvision eyepiece

Assault rifle with laser to track moving targets

Risky business

Spying is not restricted to military and government secrets. Companies, engineers and designers are under attack from spies trying to steal their ideas or information.

Under wraps

Companies often hire spies to collect information on new products and innovations. They also try to guard their own secrets as closely as possible. This is called *corporate espionage.*

This new car model is being road tested. The manufacturers try to disguise various design features.

A camouflage wrap disguises the car's body shape from long-range cameras.

Tape hides the design of lights, window frames and other parts.

False padding changes the look of grills and wheel arches.

Internet raiders

Business groups have to protect their information from spies known as *hackers* – computer experts who can infiltrate data files using an internet connection.

Not all hackers are a serious threat. In 2002, UK civilian Gary Mackinnon was caught hacking CIA files, but he was only hunting for information about UFO sightings.

The enemy within

Counter-intelligence officers, or *counter-spies*, need to stay alert to the threat of spies inside their own agencies. They can test loyalty through an operation known as a *sting*. Here's how it works...

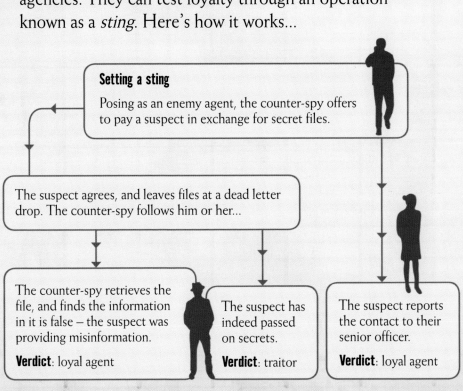

Setting a sting

Posing as an enemy agent, the counter-spy offers to pay a suspect in exchange for secret files.

The suspect agrees, and leaves files at a dead letter drop. The counter-spy follows him or her...

The counter-spy retrieves the file, and finds the information in it is false – the suspect was providing misinformation.

Verdict: loyal agent

The suspect has indeed passed on secrets.

Verdict: traitor

The suspect reports the contact to their senior officer.

Verdict: loyal agent

Spy kit 5: present and future

Modern spies have access to a wealth of new technology. It allows them to collect ever more information, and gives them the means to hide it and send it around the world in secret.

Sky scanners

Radar domes help military agencies scan huge areas of the sky, giving them early warning of missile attacks.

Many new espionage devices are developed by a US agency known as IARPA: Intelligence Advanced Research Projects Activity.

These three domes are located at RAF Fylingdales in Yorkshire, UK. They can detect any missiles launched inside Europe.

Mathematical codes

Computer scientists have developed a system known as *quantum key distribution*, that allows spies to create ultra safe codes.

In the field

A ◄ – – – – – – – – – – – – – ► B

1. Spy A sends the day's new code in an email to spy B.

2. If a hacker tries to access the code, the numbers in the code change. So spies A and B know it's not safe to use that code again.

Face finders

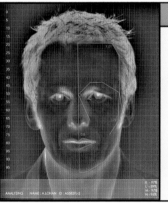

Facial-recognition cameras help spies to hunt and track suspects on city streets.

Computers use cameras to map out specific parts of a face, and automatically compare them to faces on a database.

In the field

Invisible vehicles

Engineers have developed fabrics called *metamaterials*, that can bend and reflect certain forms of light.

They are still testing ways to coat large objects, such as cars, in metamaterials.

In development

Light bends around the object, so the viewer can't see it.

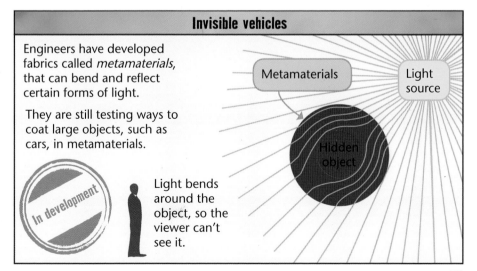

Metamaterials

Light source

Hidden object

Truth and fiction

Spies have always been popular action heroes in movies and books. Some of the most famous characters in spy stories were created by real life espionage agents.

Ian Fleming (UK, 1908–1964)

Fleming was recruited by Naval Intelligence during the Second World War. He drew on the personalities and exploits of SOE and MI6 officers to create secret agent James Bond.

Fleming enjoyed a lifestyle almost as glamorous as Bond's. He raced sports cars, lived on a private estate in Jamaica, and wrote on a gold typewriter.

John le Carré (UK, 1931–present)

British spy David Cornwall worked for both MI5 and MI6 during the height of the Cold War. In his time at MI6, he wrote two spy novels, adopting the pen name John le Carré to protect his true identity.

Since leaving the service, he has written 22 further spy novels, many featuring soft-spoken MI6 agent George Smiley.

How to become a spy

Believe it or not, most intelligence agencies post job information on their own websites – you just have to see what is available, and be old enough to apply.

Spies on the internet

For links to websites where you can find out more about spies, intelligence agencies and the very latest in espionage technology, go to the Usborne Quicklinks website at **www.usborne.com/quicklinks** and enter the keyword: **spying**.

Around 20,000 people work for the CIA – the US Central Intelligence Agency. Their roles range from office-based analysts and administrators to international field agents.

Glossary

This glossary explains some of the words used in this book. If a word is written in *italic* type, it has an entry of its own.

bug A miniature hidden microphone.

CIA The Central Intelligence Agency, a US agency responsible for gathering *intelligence* from overseas.

cipher A message in which letters, words and numbers have been rearranged to disguise the contents.

code A method of disguising a message by swapping whole words for their own symbols.

Cold War A period of rivalry and military tension between the USA and its allies, and the Soviet Union and its allies, lasting from around 1945-1990.

control officer The officer in charge of managing a team of spies, especially as part of a *spy ring*.

counter-espionage Any work done to interfere with enemy *espionage*.

counter-intelligence Spreading *misinformation*, and any other work done to keep enemies from gaining useful *intelligence*.

counter-terrorism Work done to detect, track and stop *terrorist* groups.

cover A false name and profession used by *field agents* to protect their real identity.

dead letter drop A secret location where spies can leave messages for each other.

decipher To translate a *coded* or *ciphered* message into *plaintext*.

defector Anyone who leaves his or her country to live and work in an enemy nation.

department A section of an *agency* responsible for a particular aspect of *espionage*, such as code breaking.

double agent A spy who passes secrets to an enemy *agency*, but is secretly loyal to their own agency.

drone An unmanned vehicle, such as a spy plane, operated by remote control.

Enigma A cipher machine used by the German military during the Second World War.

espionage Anything to do with spy work or *intelligence* gathering.

FBI The Federal Bureau of Investigation, a US *agency* charged with tackling enemy activity within the USA.

field agent A spy who works outside of an *agency* building, often in enemy territory.

GCHQ The Goverment Communications Headquarters, a UK agency responsible for providing intelligence based on enemy communications, such as intercepted phone calls or emails.

hacker Someone who uses a computer to infiltrate an organization's computer files, often to steal secrets.

intelligence Reliable information about the strengths, weaknesses and activites of other countries and organizations.

Intelligence agency An *espionage* organization, such as the *CIA*.

intelligence agent Someone who works for an *Intelligence Agency* as part of a spy team. Sometimes called an intelligence officer.

KGB The Soviet Union's Committee for State Security, from 1954-1991.

legend A life story created to make a *cover* identity more believable, often backed up with false documents.

MI5 Military Intelligence section 5, another name for the UK Security Service. This organization is responsibile for protecting the country from attacks inside the UK.

MI6 see *SIS*.

misinformation False *intelligence* deliberately supplied to an enemy organization.

mole A spy who has been inserted into, or recruited from within, an enemy organization.

plaintext Any message not written in *code* or scrambled by a *cipher*.

reconnaissance Work done to map and discover information about enemy territory and movements.

sabotage Destruction of enemy targets.

saboteur An agent responsible for carrying out a *sabotage* mission.

SIS The UK Secret Intelligence Service, also known as MI6. The agency responsible for gathering *intelligence*, especially from overseas.

sleeper A spy who lives in a foreign country for years before beginning an *espionage* mission.

Special Forces Highly trained soldiers and sailors called to complete the most difficult and dangerous missions.

spy ring A team of spies working for a *control officer*. They may or may not know each other.

sting An operation to expose a traitor within an *intelligence agency*.

surveillance The art of watching and following a person or group of suspects.

terrorist A person who kills people, or blows things up, to make people afraid – often for a political reason.

UAV Unmanned Aerial Vehicle, a drone spy plane.

Index

A agencies, 5, 6, 10-11
analysts, 9, 11
Ancient Greece, 16
Ancient Rome, 16
assassination, 23, 61
atomic bomb, the, 48, 49

B Babington, Sir Anthony, 25
Baden-Powell, Robert, 17
balloons, 56
Berlin, 50-51, 59
Berlin Wall, the, 50, 51
bin Laden, Osama, 68, 69
black chamber, 20, 34
Black Hawk, 69
Bletchley Park, 44-45
Bond, James, 74
Boyd, Belle, 29
British army, 13, 17, 33
bugs, 13, 14, 60

C *cabinet noir*, 20
cameras, 12, 15, 56, 62, 64, 65
Chapman, Eddie, 46
CIA, 50, 54-55, 56, 57, 58, 59, 67, 68, 75
ciphers, 19, 21, 25, 43
Civil War, the (US), 28-29
codebreakers 11, 34, 44-45
codes, 9, 18, 20, 25, 28, 42, 43, 73
Cold War, the, 48-61
computers, 45, 64, 71, 73
control officers, 6, 11, 52, 53
corporate espionage, 70
counter-espionage, 5
counter-intelligence, 5, 9
counter-spies, 71
counter-terrorism, 68
Cuban missile crisis, 57

D DARPA, 63
databases, 27, 73
dead letter drop, 9, 52, 71
deciphering, 21, 44, 45
disguises, 7
double agents, 6, 9, 46
drones, 62, 63

E East Germany, 50, 51
Elizabeth I, 24, 25
Enigma, 43-45
escape kit, 58
extraction, 67

F FBI, 37, 59
Fermor, Patrick Leigh, 39
field agents, 7, 8, 11, 66, 67
First World War, the, 30-34
Fleming, Ian, 74
France, 20, 31, 44
Fuchs, Klaus, 49

G gadgets, 14-15, 40, 60
GCHQ, 10-11
German army, 39, 43, 46, 47
Germany, 30, 31, 34, 38, 39, 44, 45

H hackers, 71
Hannibal, 22
Hashashin, 23
helicopters, 14, 15, 66, 69
HUMINT, 5

I IARPA, 72
infiltration, 7
insertion, 66
intelligence officers, 5, 13
invisible inks, 16, 35

J jetpack, 66

Joint Intelligence Committee, 10
Julius Caesar, 19

K KGB, 36, 37, 53, 59

L lasers, 14, 69
Lawrence, T. E., 32-33
le Carré, John, 74

M Markov, Georgi, 61
Mary, Queen of Scots, 25
Mata Hari, see Zelle, Margarethe
MI5, 10-11, 49, 74
MI6, *see* SIS
moles, 6, 50, 51
Moss, W. Stanley, 39

N Navajo code, 42
night vision, 69
ninja, 23
NKVD, 36, 37, 53
nuclear missiles, 57

O Operation Mincemeat, 47

P Philby, Kim, 53
Pinkertons, the, 26-27
pochteca, 23
Powers, Gary, 59

R radar, 62, 72
radio, 38, 42, 43
reconnaissance, 12
Royal Navy, 34, 39, 47
    Naval Intelligence, 47, 74
RQ-170 Sentinel, 12
RQ-4 Global Hawk

S sabotage, 9, 30, 31
satellites, 56, 65
scytales, 22

Second World War, the, 38-47
security cameras, 7, 15, 64
Security Service, *see* MI5
SIGINT, 5
SIS, 4, 10-11, 50, 51, 53, 74
sleeper agents, 6
Smiley, George, 74
SOE, 38-41, 53
Soviet Union, the, 36, 37, 48, 49,
    53, 56, 57
Spartans, 22
Special Forces, 69
spy planes, 12, 31, 56, 57, 59, 62
spy ring, 52, 53
Stasi, the, 51
steganography, 16-17
sting, 71
submarines, 31, 63
surveillance, 8, 11, 14-15, 62, 64-65

T tapping, 28, 31, 68
TECHINT, 5
telegraphs, 28, 30, 31, 34
torture, 20
Tubman, Harriet, 29
Turkey, 32, 33

U U2 plane, 56, 57, 59
UK, 4, 10, 30, 31, 32, 34, 38, 44,
    45, 53, 74,
US army, 42
USA, 26, 28, 37, 48, 54, 57

V van, 64-65

W Walsingham, Sir Francis, 24-25

Z Zelle, Margaretha, 35
Zigzag, see Chapman, Eddie
Zimmermann, Arthur, 34

Acknowledgements

Every effort has been made to trace and acknowledge ownership of copyright. If any rights have been omitted, the publishers offer to rectify this in any future editions following notification. The publishers are grateful to the following individuals and organizations for permission to reproduce material on the following pages: (t=top, b=bottom, r=right, l=left)

cover © Tim Tadder / Corbis; **p1** © Monalyn Gracia / Corbis; **p2-3** © Harry Kerr / Getty Images; **p4-5** © David Osborn / Loop Images / Corbis; **p6-7** © Alan Schein Photography / Corbis; **p13** © Imperial War Museum (Q50942); **p17** © Steve Gallagher Photography / cultura / Corbis; **p18** © Hulton-Deutsch Collection / Corbis; **p20** (**t**) © Mary Evans Picture Library; (**b**) © Bettmann / Corbis; **p24-25** © National Maritime Museum, Greenwich, London; **p26** (**b**) © Medford Historical Society Collection / Corbis; **p27** © Bettmann / Corbis; **p29** (**t**) © Bettmann /Corbis; (**b**) © The Print Collector / Alamy; **p34** © Everett Collection Historical / Alamy; **p35** © Mondadori via Getty Images; **p36** © Mark Sykes Moscow / Alamy; **p37** © Time & Life Pictures / Getty Images; **p40** (**bl**) © INTERFOTO / Alamy; (**br**) © Imperial War Museum (EPH10115); **p42** © Corbis; **p43** © Chris Howes / Wild Places Photography / Alamy; **p44-45** © SSPL via Getty Images; **p45** © Pictorial Press Ltd / Alamy; **p48** © Corbis; **p50** © Gamma-Rapho via Getty Images; **p51** © William Durie / Demotix / Corbis; **p53** (**t**) © Bettmann / Corbis; (**b**) © Popperfoto / Getty; **p56** © NASA - digital version copyright / Science Faction / Corbis; **p57** © Bettmann / Corbis; **p58** (**t**) © Cristian Baitg / Getty; (**b**) courtesy of the International Spy Museum, Washington D.C.; **p59** (**t**) © Hulton-Deutsch Collection / Corbis; (**b**) © Bettmann / Corbis; **p62** © Time & Life Pictures / Getty Images; **p63** © Paul Wootton / Science Photo Library; **p66** © Barcroft Media via Getty Images; **p69** (**t**) model of Blackhawk helicopter from turbosquid.com, based on the design by Sikorsky Aircraft; (**b**) © MILpictures by Tom Weber via Getty Images; **p70** © Phil Crean / Alamy; **p72** © John Slater / Corbis; **p73** © Image Source /Corbis; **p74** (**t**) © Hulton-Deutsch Collection / Corbis; (**b**) © Antonin Kratochvil / VII / Corbis; **p75** © Larry Downing / Reuters / Corbis.

Additional illustrations by Anna Gould, Helen Edmonds, Zoe Wray and Ian McNee
Series editor: Jane Chisholm   Series designer: Zoe Wray
Digital design by John Russell   Picture research by Ruth King